True Colors

A VERY SEXY, VERY GAY COLORING BOOK

DESIGNED BY
ALLEN CUTLER

Published by Unzipped Books
An imprint of Lethe Press
lethepressbooks.com

Copyright © 2019 Allen Cutler

ISBN: 978-1-59021-136-6

No part of this work may be reproduced or utilized in any form or by any means, electronic or mechanical, including photocopying, microfilm, and recording, or by any information storage and retrieval system, without permission in writing from the Author or Publisher. All designs are from the artist's imagination and any resemblance to persons living or dead is purely coincidental.

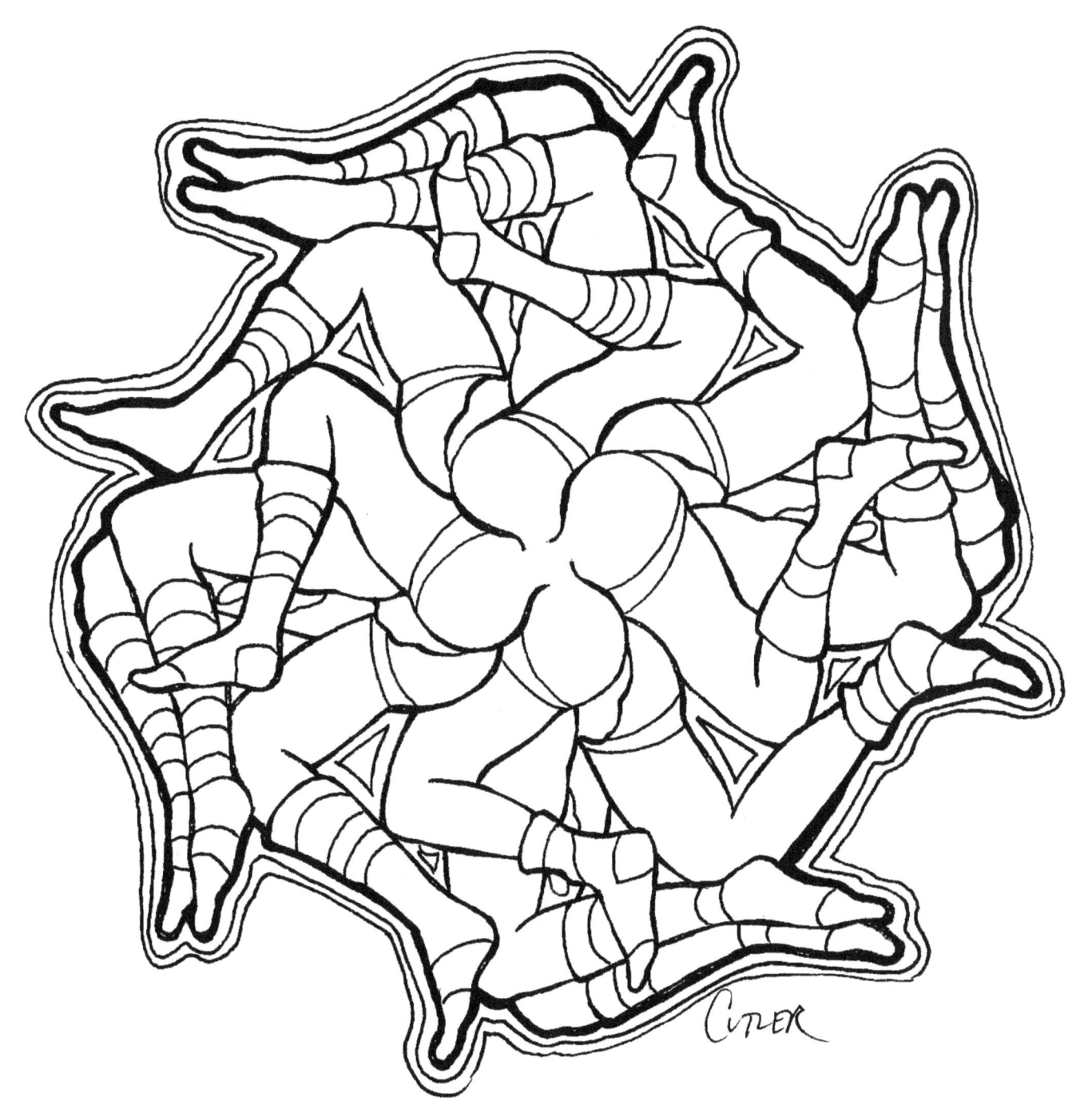

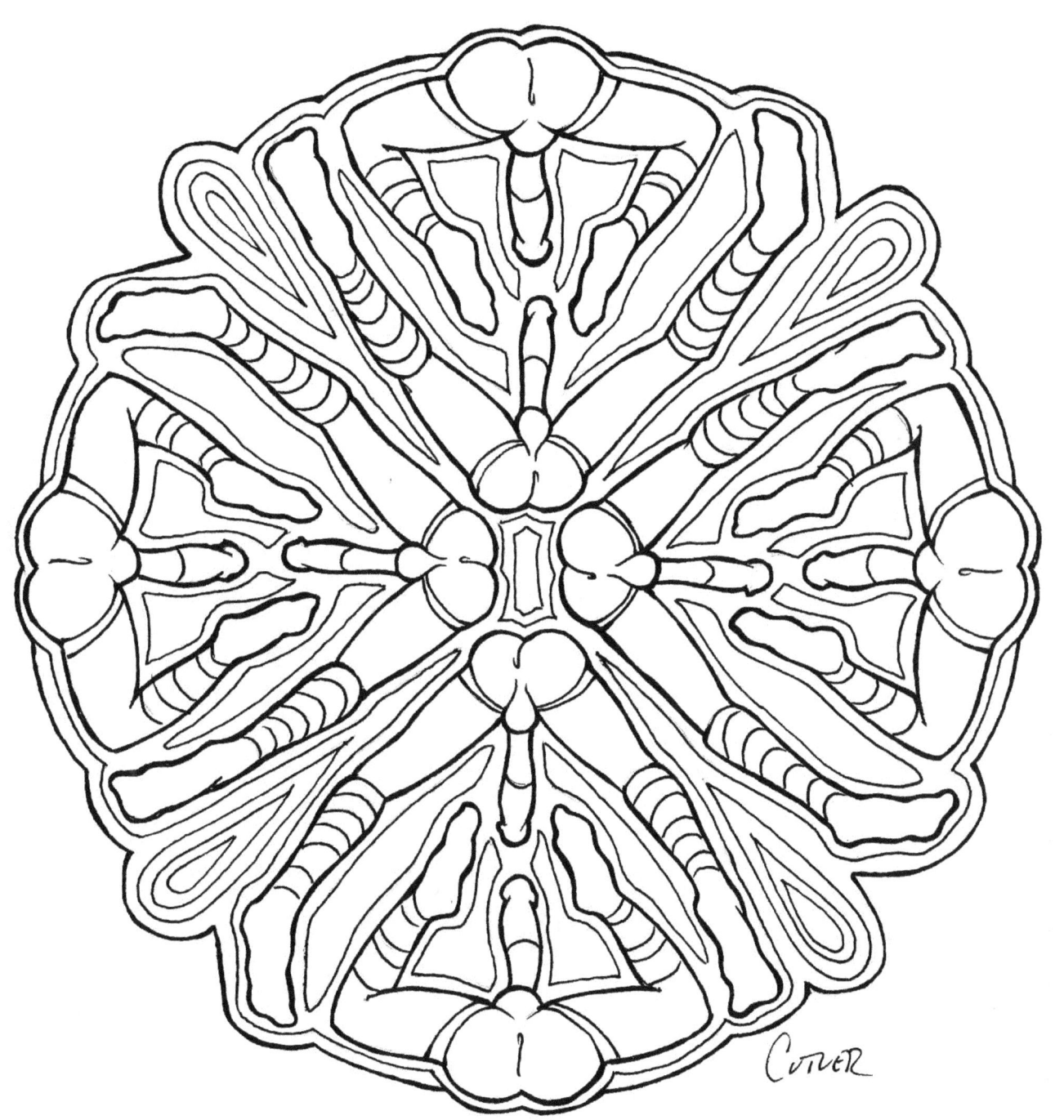

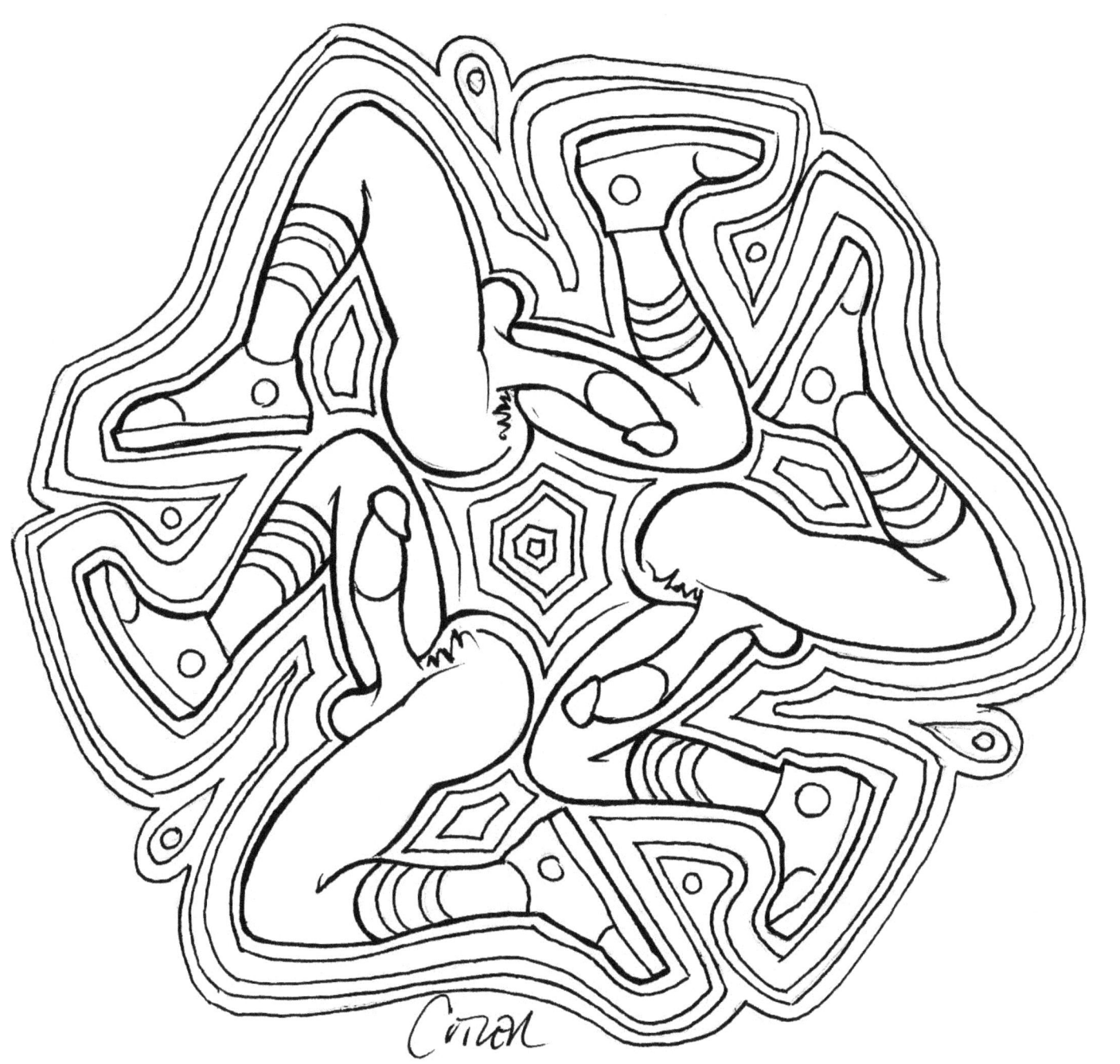

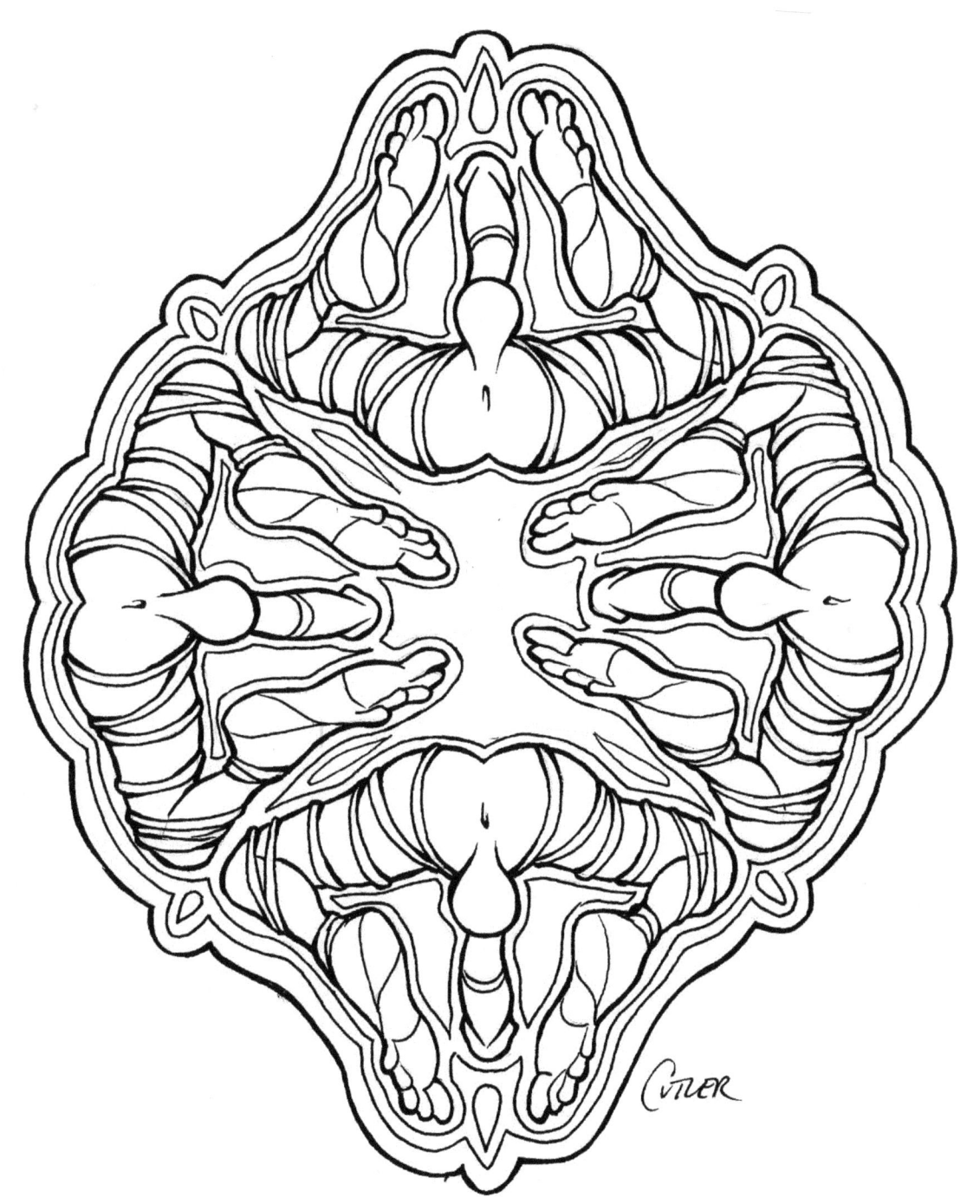

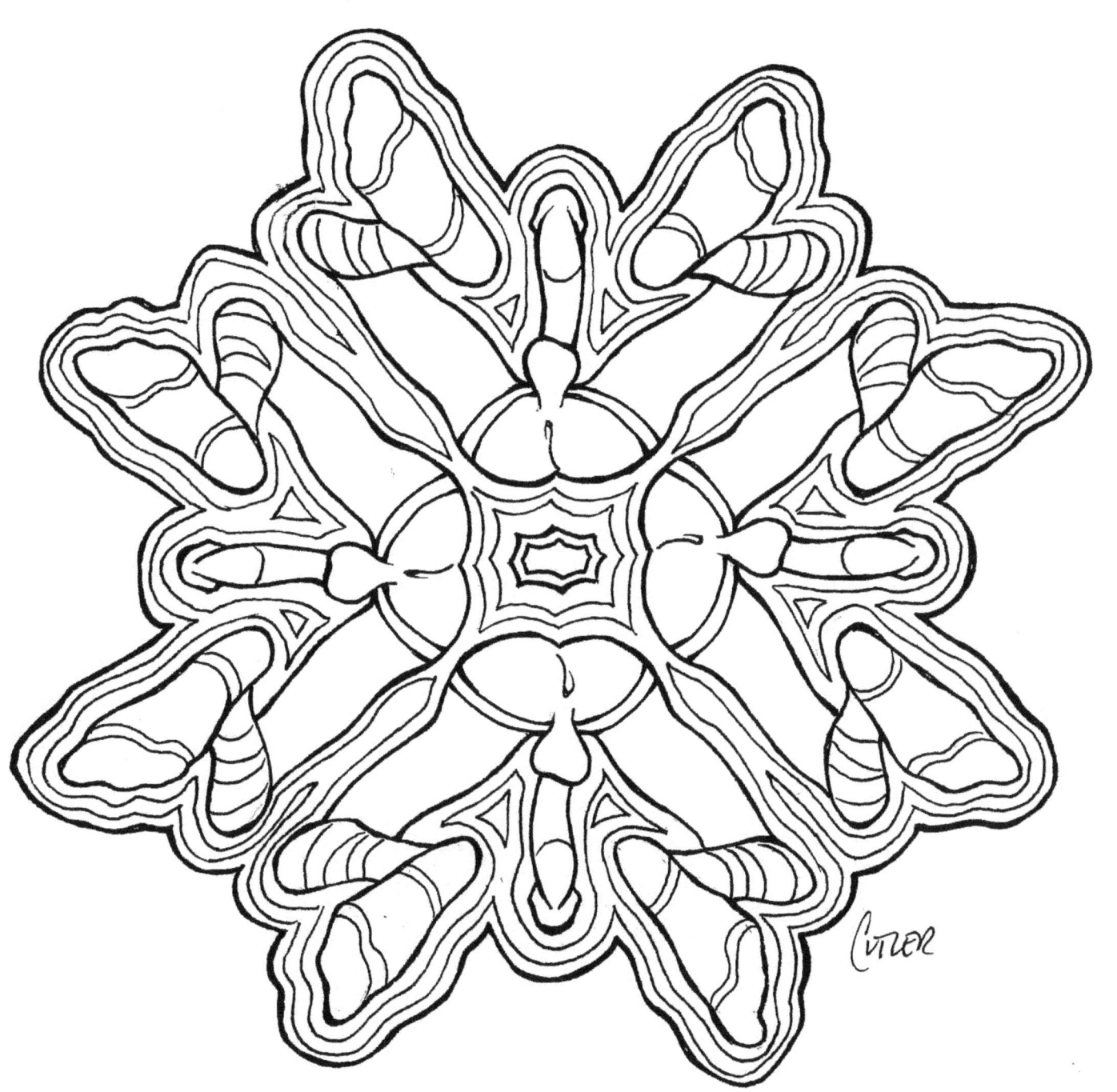

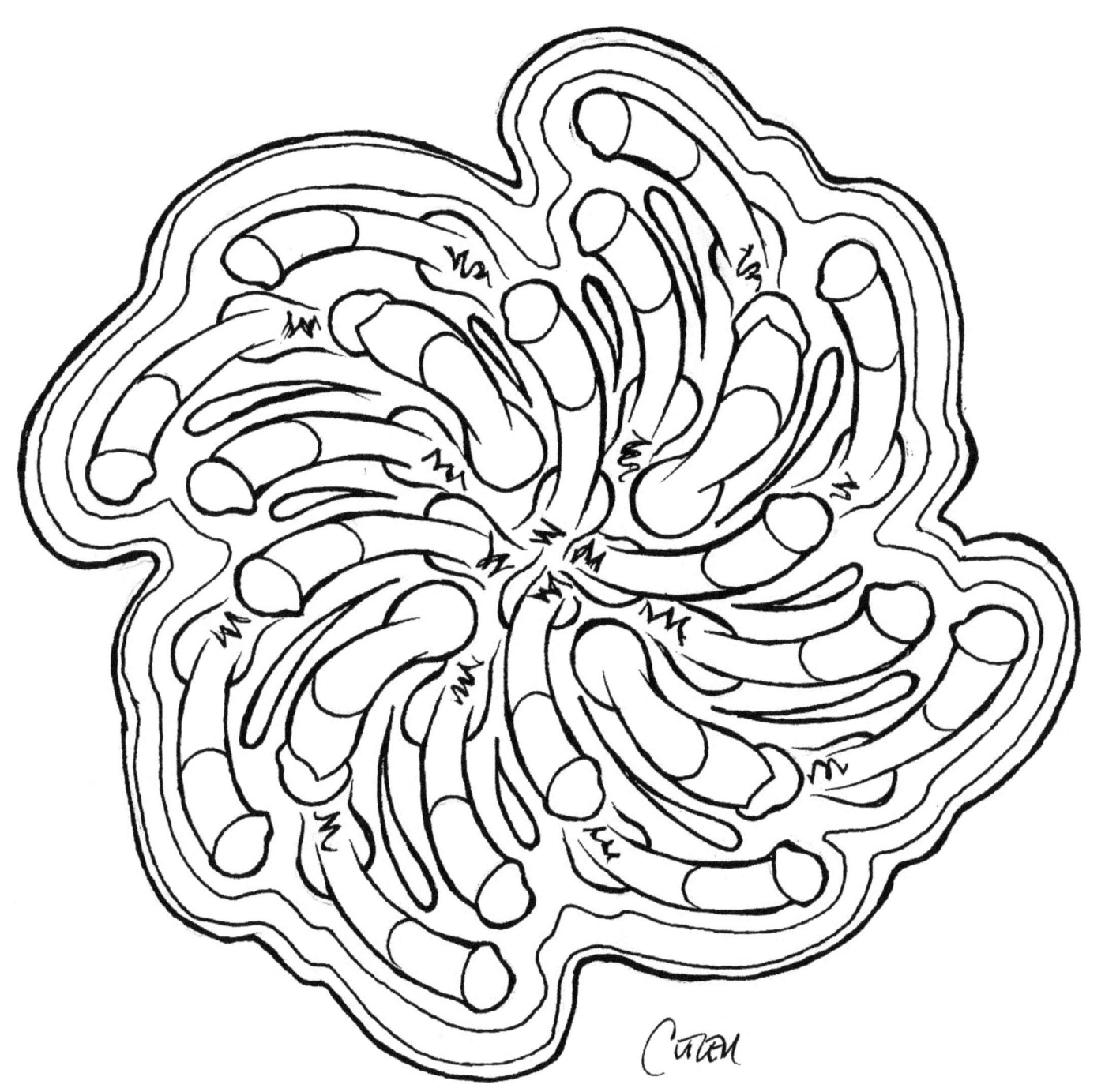

ALLEN CUTLER is a self-taught artist who works mostly in embroidery exploring the homoerotic, sex, and the male body. His work has been seen at Art+Party Drama League NY, NY, The Rochester Erotic Arts Festival Rochester, NY, Stitch Fetish 7 at The Hive Gallery Los Angeles, CA, Mercury@Machinewerks Seattle, WA and The Seattle Erotic Art Festival Seattle, WA where he was awarded the Foundation Award when his work was added to the permanent collection of the Pan Eros Foundation. His work is in many private collections, including that of performer Sam Smith and Lethe Press owner Steve Berman. You can find his work on Instagram @eroticneedle.

www.ingramcontent.com/pod-product-compliance
Lightning Source LLC
Chambersburg PA
CBHW081020040426
42444CB00014B/3284